D0728497

Conflict and
Communication
in the Family Business

Joseph H. Astrachan, Ph. D. and
Kristi S. McMillan

Family Business Leadership Series, No. 16

Family Enterprise Publishers
P.O. Box 4356
Marietta, GA 30061-4356
800-551-0633
www.efamilybusiness.com

ISSN: 1071-5010
ISBN: 1-891652-10-9

Family Business Leadership Series

We believe that family businesses are special, not only to the families that own and manage them but to our society and to the private enterprise system. Having worked and interacted with hundreds of family enterprises in the past twenty years, we offer the insights of that experience and the collected wisdom of the world's best and most successful family firms.

This volume is a part of a series offering practical guidance for family businesses seeking to manage the special challenges and opportunities confronting them.

To order additional copies, contact:
Family Enterprise Publishers
1220-B Kennestone Circle
Marietta, Georgia 30066
Tel: 1-800-551-0633
Web Site: www.efamilybusiness.com

Quantity discounts are available.

Other volumes in the series include:

Family Business Succession: The Final Test of Greatness, 2nd ed.

Family Meetings: How to Build a Stronger Family and a Stronger Business, 2nd ed.

Another Kind of Hero: Preparing Successors for Leadership

How Families Work Together

Family Business Compensation

How to Choose and Use Advisors: Getting the Best Professional Family Business Advice

Financing Transitions: Managing Capital and Liquidity in the Family Business

Family Business Governance: Maximizing Family and Business Potential

Preparing Your Family Business for Strategic Change

Making Sibling Teams Work: The Next Generation

Developing Family Business Policies: Your Guide to the Future

Family Business Values: How to Assure a Legacy of Continuity and Success

More Than Family: Non-Family Executives in the Family Business

Make Change Your Family Business Tradition

Family Business Ownership: How To Be An Effective Shareholder

Contents

Exhibits

I. Introduction: Understanding Conflict and Communication

Nothing distresses a business-owning family as much as conflict among family members, or frustrates it so much as the inability of family members to communicate with one another satisfactorily. We see the signs of people's exasperation over conflict and communication issues in such questions and comments as:

— "Why can't our sons and daughters get along? We're afraid to pass our business on to them because they just keep fighting with one another."

— "Why won't Dad listen to me?"

— "My sister was always Mom's favorite. Now look at her. She gets to run the company and I'm supposed to take orders from her."

— "Let's face it. My brother can't be trusted. I couldn't trust him when I was a kid and I can't trust him now."

The conflicts and feelings that lie beneath the surface of these statements can undo a family if they are not addressed. And, as we all know, they often tear family businesses apart as well. Recent history is filled with instances of family companies that failed to make it to the next generation because family members couldn't resolve their differences and communicate successfully with one another. In a 1995 survey of 800 heirs of failed family businesses, conflict with family members in and out of the business and with non-family employees was viewed as a major cause of business failure. In another study of 673 businesses, a clear relationship was found between decreased family tension and increased business revenues.

In one of the most famous and heartbreaking cases, the Bingham family of Louisville, Kentucky, felt forced to sell its greatly admired media empire in 1986 in large part because the third-generation siblings could not overcome the mutual distrust and disrespect that had taken root in childhood. Much of the blame for the Bingham's failure to resolve their conflicts was laid to family members' inability to communicate with one another.

Obviously, you don't want your family and your business to suffer a similar fate. Conflict, as inevitable as it is and as healthy

Recent history is filled with instances of family companies that failed to make it to the next generation because family members couldn't resolve their differences and communicate successfully with one another.

Conflict can poison a family and its business.

as it can sometimes be, can poison a family and its business. Its antidote is good communication. In this case, however, the antidote is best applied before the poisoning occurs—somewhat like administering a vaccine before exposure to a disease. But once in place, while often painful, open communication is the only long-term cure apart from divine intervention or extraordinary luck.

Good communication doesn't eliminate conflict but it does help you manage it effectively so that it does not become poisonous, overly emotional, and destructive. Good relationships depend on common goals being stronger than conflicting goals and this can only be assured through good communication. Business-owning families that do not resolve conflict through communication risk dangers ranging from litigation, to the dissolution of the business, to the painful and dishonorable destruction of the family.

This book is intended to help you avoid such perils. It shows you how to discern what conflict really is and offer guidance for dealing with the emotional content that lies beneath it. It provides you with an understanding of some very common dynamics that surround conflict. It explains how communication works and how you can make it better. And it offers ideas for improving your negotiation skills and suggests strategies for coping with difficult family members. You will also come to a better understanding of your family's communication patterns and gain insight into how a person's power or position in the family affects their personal communication style.

You are encouraged to share this book with other members of your family. When everyone is working together to improve communication skills and manage conflict, the chances of success are much greater, and the family becomes closer and more unified. Nevertheless, if you are in a family where you must "go it alone" on conflict and communication issues, this book offers support.

If you are a non-family member of a family business or on a board of directors, you will also find value in these pages. This book helps you better understand the dynamics of the business-owning family and should enable you to serve the business more effectively. If you are a non-family employee, it helps you unscramble some of the puzzling messages that can emerge in a family company and aids you in avoiding misinterpretation. You will learn to better recognize the difference between an order and a question. When the boss says, "Wouldn't this room look good painted red?," you'll know whether she wants you to have the

Good communication doesn't eliminate conflict but it does help you manage it effectively so that it does not become poisonous, overly emotional, and destructive.

room painted red or if she's just speculating on what it might look like.

What distinguishes this book from other material you may have read on the subject is that it emphasizes *family* communication and shows what goes on beneath the surface of *family* conflict. You will see what happens when the family spills over into the business, and that the resolution of conflict through good communication, while it affects the business, must come from within the family.

Family members often fear that talking about difficult matters only makes things worse. On the contrary, it's NOT talking about those difficult issues that make things worse. It is the intent of this book to demystify the risks of communication and to show that the dangers of not talking are much greater than the risks of communicating effectively. Communication skills can be learned and you have made a good start by picking up this book.

II. The Many Masks of Conflict

Conflict is a complex notion, and it may not be what many people think it is. When we hear the word "conflict," we often think of a physical fight or a verbal one: Two men engaged in fisticuffs in a boxing ring or on a street corner. A husband and wife shouting angrily at each other. Two women's teams vying with each other on a soccer field. Armies battling each other in the mountains. The endless conflict in the Middle East, with its detonation of suicide bombs by one side and deadly retaliation by another.

To be sure, conflict can be contentious and it can be defined as war or struggle or battle. But conflict in a family business is often much more subtle. It can be hidden or denied. It is sometimes quiet. It may be so invisible that people inside and outside the family don't recognize it's there. It almost always hides deeper issues.

Conflict is the perception of irreconcilable goals. Notice that emotion is not a necessary part of conflict—emotionality, hurt and anger come when people begin to recognize that conflict exists. In *The Playwright's Guidebook*, dramatist and teacher Stuart Spencer writes: "Conflict is that which prevents a character from getting what he or she wants." He warns that conflict should not be confused with emotion, action or argument. While conflict can involve fighting and confrontation and yelling, says Spencer, they are "not the essence of what conflict actually is." Conflict, he points out, can be poignant and subdued, as in a scene where a teen-age girl tries to prevent her younger sister from going outside to play hopscotch by convincing her it's more important to stay inside and do her homework. The little sister has an incurable illness and the older one is trying to protect her, but they both want different things: one to go outdoors, the other to save her sister's life. The older girl does not share the real reason for her position.

Surface Issues

In many cases, in family business, conflict emerges from the love and caring that family members have for one another—like the sisters in the play. Many other cases, however, are not so benign. And while Spencer says conflict is not to be confused with emotion, it's important to understand that conflict can cause excruciating emotions.

On the surface, disagreement appears to be centered on obvious issues that need to be negotiated. Typical among them are:

—**Compensation.** What are family members working in the business paid? What bonuses should they receive? What dividends should family shareholders be entitled to?

—Entry and promotion. What family members are permitted to work in the business? Who among them will be promoted? Who will run the company once Mom or Dad retires?

—Ownership. Who gets to own and who doesn't? How many shares can a family member own and how much power will ownership give to a particular individual? Keep in mind, that, while things are changing rapidly, tradition in many business families has prevented daughters from becoming owners. In some families, only members who work in the business are permitted to own shares. In most families, who can own is not discussed or decided until the conflict is in full swing.

—Communication. This is expressed in such comments as: "You never tell me anything!" "You leave me out of the loop." "You talk to my people without talking to me." "You talk behind my back."

—How the grandchildren are treated. Does an adult son feel that his parents are ignoring his own children while lavishing attention on his sibling's kids?

While these issues deserve attention in and of themselves, they are usually signs of deeper, difficult issues that a family must eventually uncover and deal with in order to ease or resolve surface conflict. The surface concerns mask such underlying issues as:

—Feelings of not being taken seriously. When a family member believes her parents or siblings fail to regard her with adequate respect, she often makes comments like: "You don't understand me." "I'm an adult now." "You're not listening to me." Some people might call these concerns the issues of "delayed adolescence," but they don't go away.

—The need for parental love. Every child wants to be loved and recognized by the parents—even when the children are adults. When children do not feel loved, or feel less loved than their siblings, their relationships with their parents and brothers and sisters can be marred for a lifetime.

—Lack of trust. Distrust can be rooted in childhood and sometimes goes back for generations. A child can tell a sibling, "I don't trust you!" and still feel that way in adulthood. Distrust is expressed in such statements as, "You have a different agenda than I do," or, "You don't care about me. You're in it for yourself." When distrust was born in a previous generation, one young adult family member may tell a cousin: "Three generations ago, your great-grandfather stiffed my great-grandfather for the presidency of the company. I just don't trust your family branch. You only look out for yourselves."

—Favoritism. The surface issue of how grandparents treat the grandchildren often masks the issue of how the senior generation treated their own children. A son may have felt that his brother got all the parents' attention when they were kids but couldn't bring himself to say so to his parents then. Now he expresses himself by complaining to his parents about how they are shortchanging his children. What he really means, however, is that they shortchanged him.

—**Fairness.** Family members want to be treated fairly, although their views of fairness may differ. The matter of compensation among siblings offers a classic example. One may feel that fairness means all receive equal pay—especially if she sees equal treatment as a sign of family togetherness. Another may believe that fairness means compensation is based on merit—especially if he feels he is contributing more to the business and is "carrying" the others.

The Bingham family mentioned in the Introduction offers an example of several of these underlying issues. The family owned the highly regarded Louisville *Courier-Journal* and other media holdings. But the family conflicts were brought to a head by Sallie Bingham, a daughter in the third generation. It has been reported that she grew up distrusting her two older brothers—especially the heir apparent, whose death in an accident disrupted plans for the future of the family's business. Feeling that she was neither loved nor taken seriously by her family, Sallie became vocal and demanded to be listened to and taken seriously, eventually suing to redeem her shares of the company. In tragic desperation and despair, not being willing or able to confront the ceaseless bickering, Barry Bingham Sr., the patriarch and controlling shareholder, finally decided to sell the company to outsiders.

The Patterns of Conflict

Conflict is made more complicated by the fact that different families have different cycles, or patterns, of conflict—often the result of cultural background. Exhibit 1 below shows how the cycles work in different kinds of families. "Enmeshed" families, where members get very involved in each others' lives, experience a frequent number of emotional ups and downs in a given day—bursting into conflict perhaps every three or four hours. Their conflicts are likely to contain a great deal of "emotional heat." Sometimes such families are so used to this, that they may not give it a second thought. Enmeshed families are often Mediterranean, Hispanic, Jewish, or have in their history a prior generation forced to live in close quarters or in significant isolation.

In the other extreme, "distant families," typically Anglo-Saxon or Northern European, might have a conflict cycle that stretches out over a period of months and that reaches a peak only three or four times a year.

Conflict is made more complicated by the fact that different families have different cycles, or patterns, of conflict— often the result of cultural background.

EXHIBIT 1

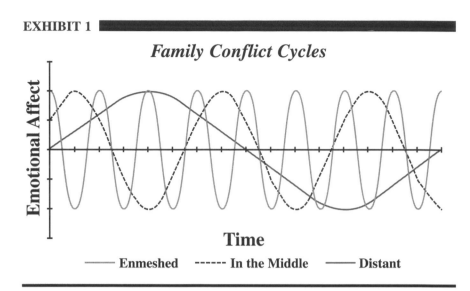

Family Conflict Cycles

Emotional Affect

Time

——— **Enmeshed**   ------ **In the Middle**   ——— **Distant**

One study asked 600 family business participants how often conflicts occurred for them. Weekly, said 20 percent; monthly, said another 20 percent; and 42 percent said three to five times a year.

There's no "right" or "wrong" pattern. What feels normal to someone who grew up in an Italian immigrant family may seem intolerable to a New Englander with a Scottish background. Of special relevance to family businesses in this respect is the matter of in-laws. If your family has a three-hour conflict cycle, imagine how difficult it can be when your brother, Emilio, weds his English fiancée, Pamela, who is used to a family that argues openly only about once every two months. It may make no sense to her that you are all getting angry at each other and getting happy again all in one stroke, because in her family, when people get mad, it lasts, and then when they get happy again, it lasts.

As Exhibit 2 shows, events can profoundly influence conflict cycles. While the peaks and valleys of a family's cycle remain the same distance apart, the peaks

Events can profoundly influence conflict cycles.

are higher and the valleys lower during difficult times but more shallow when times are good. In other words, emotionalism of the conflict can increase or decrease dramatically, depending on the environment. If your family is stable, its members get along with one another, and succession is proceeding well, then the conflict is muted. However, if your company is facing bankruptcy and the founder has just died, you can expect your family to go through some really angry, mean, unhappy times. But when the triggering events are past, family members tend to feel better than they did before.

EXHIBIT 2

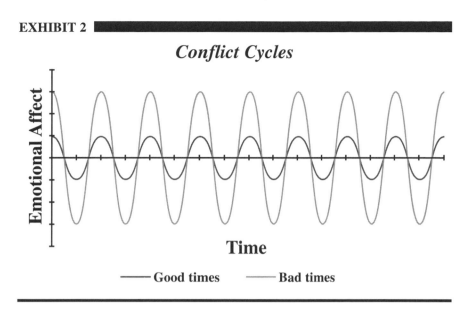

Conflict Cycles

Emotional Affect

Time

―――― Good times ―――― Bad times

This discussion isn't meant to imply that Emilio shouldn't marry Pamela. The important thing is for family members to understand their own family's conflict patterns and to make allowances for other cycles as marriages occur and in-laws are brought into the picture. It is also helpful to recognize the impact of outside events on these patterns and to be prepared for the fact that stressful times tend to exacerbate conflict. Armed with such knowledge, family members can more readily step back from a conflict, saying, "This really isn't personal."

When Conflict Is Denied

"We never fight," claims one family business CEO. "The kids get along. They understand their roles in the business and that Jimmy's going to take over some day. They're happy. We've got nothing to fight about."

But is that true? Or, is dad just a heavy lid on an explosive situation? Sometimes families think they have no conflict because the conflict is so suppressed. In our experience, conflict that is latent or denied can be much more dangerous and destructive than conflict that is in the open, where it can be managed. Let us be clear, while we advocate discussing and managing conflicts, ones that have been avoided for a long time cannot and should not be opened quickly. Such conflict needs to be handled with extreme care.

Conflict that is latent or denied can be much more dangerous and destructive than conflict that is in the open, where it can be managed.

Some people think they have good relationships when in fact they don't. "My brother and I have a great relationship," a family business member declares. But when you explore with him what that means, you discover that he and his sibling rarely talk, and when they do, the conversations last about 30 seconds. The lack of interaction actually covers the fact that these brothers are not really relating to each other at all. They want to believe they have a good relationship, and they let their short interactions lead them to believe it is so. If they would actually talk, the façade of having a good relationship would fall apart. In effect, they have "hidden the evidence" of their bad relationship. **A good relationship requires frequent interactions of reasonable duration.**

When a business-owning family allows no expression of disagreement or conflict, things are likely to explode. Often, a whistle blower will emerge, either inside the family or elsewhere in the business. Sallie Bingham is a classic example, because she wasn't listened to at a very young age, she learned to exaggerate to get people to listen. Like many people in her situation, she was regarded as eccentric, even crazy and her credibility suffered.

Conflict that is latent or denied encourages situations that are more dangerous than having an open disagreement. Talking about somebody behind their back is one example. Consider a brother who is mad at his sister. He goes off after work and talks with the shop foreman over drinks about what an idiot his sister is, even though she's in charge of the company. He complains about how she goes to a spa on company time and lets her teenage son go out on dates using a company car. The shop foreman tells other employees, and soon, people begin to leave the company because they feel the family is so screwed up. Or they say, "The family's getting away with things. I'll get away with things, too." Little by little, the circle of damage expands.

A good relationship requires frequent interactions of reasonable duration.

A Behavior Trap

The brother in the preceding anecdote is engaging in what psychologists call "passive-aggressive" behavior. People are "passive-aggressive" when they cannot bring themselves to express anger directly but instead express it through indirect action. Sometimes such behavior is unintentional—perhaps it didn't occur to the brother above that letting off steam to the wrong person could be harmful to the company. Other times, however, the behavior is intentional but the perpetrator passes it off as innocent—which can be very confusing to the person on the receiving end. Often the perpetrator truly believes it is unintentional because anger is completely unacceptable to others.

Suppose Brian, the sales manager of a family business asks his younger brother, Mark, the head of manufacturing, to meet with an important customer. Mark fails to set up the meeting, causing Brian considerable embarrassment and obstructing his ability to close the sale quickly. "I'm sorry! I forgot!" says Mark.

Did he forget? Maybe, maybe not. But he was angry at Brian for ordering him around. He dragged his feet about making the appointment, and then it just sort of got put on the back burner. If Mark felt any happiness at Brian's misfortune, he almost certainly was acting from unrecognized anger.

When you're not angry but are about to commit an act that will hurt someone, you often stop yourself, saying, "what I'm doing is going to make her mad. I shouldn't do this." But when you're angry, you're more likely to allow yourself to take the action, saying to yourself, "I don't care if it makes her angry." If you're honest with yourself, you know you want to make the other person angry. But if you're not honest with yourself, you claim you meant no harm.

In any case, passive-aggressive behavior sidesteps the real issue. In the case of Brian and Mark, Brian never understood that Mark was angry with him. Instead of expressing his anger honestly and directly, Mark avoided confrontation but gained the satisfaction of hurting Brian by making what appeared to be an innocent mistake.

"Conflicts" That Aren't Really Conflicts

Much of our work with families involves showing them that members aren't really in conflict with one another. They may think they have a disagreement when what they actually have is a communication error. They have simply communicated in ways that have led them to believe they disagree when, in fact, they don't.

We'll talk about how to correct communication errors in Chapter IV. But for now, keep in mind that **sometimes miscommunication can be interpreted as a conflict.**

The Positive Side of Conflict

Conflict has its positive aspects. Thank goodness for that, because all business-owning families experience conflict. It's a given.

Conflict offers opportunities to be creative and to strengthen human relationships. When family members work together to resolve disagreements, they often arrive at solutions that are better than what they would have come up with if they had simply compromised or if one person had given in to another. The National Center for Family Philanthropy, tells of a rift that occurred between younger and older members of the board of a family foundation, which was set up with proceeds from the sale of the family business. The younger board members wanted to funnel grants to animal rights causes while the older members had their own favorite projects, such as the United Way and the Salvation Army.

With the help of a mediator, the family came up with a way to move forward: each board member would have matching discretionary funds to use for his or her pet causes, while the rest of the foundation's grant making would be dedicated to solving hunger and educating the public about good nutrition.

It was a much more satisfactory solution

Conflict offers opportunities to be creative and to strengthen human relationships.

When everyone involved in a conflict puts in the time and the honest effort to work through to a resolution, their relationships with one another become stronger and more rewarding.

than letting the senior members of the board use their power to dominate the decision or, as almost happened, asking the younger members to resign. The conflict also resulted in a more focused and probably much more effective foundation.

More important, by working through the conflict in a civilized way, the board members prevented the family from being torn apart.

Open conflict is a sign of caring. It involves the willingness of people to get emotional with one another and to be openly angry, which is a sign of attachment that one should treasure. Someone who is willing to be angry with you is showing that they care and are concerned about you. And when everyone involved in a conflict puts in the time and the honest effort to work through to a resolution, their relationships with one another become stronger and more rewarding.

III. What Makes Good Communication So Hard?

"Don't go asking Dad if he's got a will or what he wants us to do if he becomes incapacitated," a sister in a family business warns her brother. "It'll kill him if you do."

"I just can't talk to you!" a business owner snaps at his wife. "You get too emotional."

"You say one thing and then do another!" an heir-apparent complains to his mother, CEO of the family's business.

Sound familiar? All these examples reflect communication problems typical in business-owning families. Communication is hard. Good communication is even harder. However, when communication goes well, so do personal relationships and the family business runs more smoothly.

But why is communicating so exceptionally difficult? Isn't it just a matter of one person sending a message and another receiving and understanding it? That's the basic idea, but like conflict, communication gets very complicated. All kinds of roadblocks stand in the way of the give and take that comprises communication.

Myths About Communication

Some of the barriers to mutual understanding are created by the myths many of us believe about communication. Here are two common ones:

Myth #1. Our family (or someone in it) is just too fragile to discuss sensitive issues. When family members believe this, tough topics don't get addressed, no matter how urgent the need. Often, however, this is a mistaken belief. The brother in the first example opened up the topic of his father's will and what the father wanted should he become incapacitated. And guess what? Bringing up these subjects didn't lead to the father's death—despite the daughter's dire prediction. Instead, family members all around experienced feelings of relief that at last these issues were being explored. In some cases a family member will get upset, but family members need to balance their reaction with how quickly they typically recover.

Emotion is an inherent part of conflict.

Myth #2. If we discuss this, it will only make matters worse. In fact, the opposite is usually true. Undiscussed differences fester. Like the husband in the second example above, people often fear bringing up a sensitive topic because they know the other person will get emotional. They see an emotional reaction as "making matters worse." But emotion is an inherent part of conflict. Avoiding discussion of an issue won't make the emotion go away; it only drives the emotion underground—for a time. Typically we say that other people become too emotional because we are uncomfortable in the presence of strong feelings. But, like getting used to anything, we will become more comfortable if we try hard enough.

We Communicate on Many Levels

Another factor that makes communication so difficult is that we constantly communicate on many different levels. We communicate not only through our words, whether they are spoken or written, but we "talk" to each other in non-verbal ways as well. When family members spend a great deal of time together, they can be uncannily good at reading one another. Sometimes the non-verbal messages we send are stronger than the verbal ones. If so, they can change the meaning of the words or undermine the words altogether.

Here are some of the ways we communicate both verbally and non-verbally:

—Body language. We send signals with our bodies all the time. If you look at your son with hardened eyes, you may be telling him to be quiet or that you are angry. If you lean forward in your chair and your eyes are soft, you're suggesting that you're connected and you're listening. If you roll your eyes when someone else is speaking, you're expressing exasperation or disgust.

The way you handle space is also a form of body language. If someone you're talking to is getting emotional and you listen and begin to get close that suggests an effort to comfort the other person. On the other hand, if you are yelling at someone and move in on them, you're showing dominance and signaling attack.

—Action. What we do or fail to do sends a strong message. Suppose Mom and Dad tell their son they welcome his new wife into the family with open arms. If they then treat her shabbily—criticizing the way she keeps house or neglecting to invite her for lunch when the other women in the family are getting together—that tells the son that his parents don't welcome his wife after all.

—Timing issues. These involve time and how it is used in communication. Here are some examples:

1. "Air time." How much time does each participant get to talk? If we have a 10-minute conversation and you use up 9-1/2 minutes, you're asserting your power or your lack of concern for others.

2. Timed response. If I deliberately wait to return your phone calls, I am probably conveying that your call wasn't very important to me—even if you are my brother. But if I respond quickly to a call or a question, I'm demonstrating that I care—unless I'm conveying that I'm just dismissing you or trying to get rid of you. You'll perceive the difference!

3. Pace. What happens when you speak slowly, putting more distance between words? Doing so usually commands attention; listeners hang on to your every word. Some people speak very softly to achieve the same result.

—Power and intimacy. Every communication we have carries a message about the relative power and intimacy of the sender and the receiver. A person with the most power may be patronizing ("You don't know what you're talking about.") or may convey your lower status by the way he or she controls the flow of information ("I shouldn't be telling you this, because you're not a part of the executive committee, but I'll share this with you anyway." Or, "I'm going to let you in on a little secret.").

People also convey power through non-verbal ways. If you're a person who interrupts others, that's a sign that you believe you're in the more powerful position. You may demonstrate power through your posture or through the self-confidence that you exhibit when you speak.

Intimacy has to do with how much we share of ourselves when we're communicating. A business owner may tell a key executive that it's time to make Charlie retire, saying, "He just doesn't have it anymore," showing a lower level of intimacy. Or the owner may say, "I really hate to say this but we need to ease Charlie into retirement. He was my first boss when Dad brought me into the company as a teenager. He taught me the ropes. I owe him a lot. But it's clear he's really having a tough time with the job. Let's make this as easy for him as possible."

People often speak of intimacy in terms of "temperature." The individual who shares the most intimate details is seen as a "warm" person, while someone who shares little is seen as "cold."

—Parallel conversations. There are often two or more conversations going on at one time. We might start talking about compensation, but if you read between the lines of the conversation, it could be about which of us is the more competent. At an even deeper level, it could be about "Who does Dad love more?"

—Indirect storytelling. A mother may tell an adult son about a friend of hers who forgave a family member for some wrongdoing. What the mother really wants is for her son to see that he needs to be more forgiving of his brother. Frequently people try to avoid a confrontation by telling a story about someone else, hoping that the person we're talking to will "get the message."

Communication Patterns Differ from Family to Family

Just as there are different conflict cycles in different families, there are also different patterns of communication in different families. One family may be very argumentative, with everyone jumping into the fray. Another may prefer quieter intellectual discourse or to hardly communicate at all. In still another, Dad always gets the last word. Or the kids communicate to the father through their mother, and she in turn uses the father to communicate back to the kids. Sometimes, unwilling to express herself directly, the mother may invoke the father when communicating with the children: "You know what your father always says." In some rare families, everyone's opinion is welcomed and everyone is heard.

The next generation either completely adopts a communication pattern or rejects it. If you liked the way your parents communicated, you're going to do it the same way. You're dad didn't mince words, so you don't mince words. Or, your father always beats around the bush and was very oblique and didn't say what he meant, so you don't say what you mean. Dad never treated women with respect; he talked to them as if they were subservient. In reaction, his son treats women with excessive respect (which, as a side note, can be just as dehumanizing).

Resolving conflict thoroughly and improving communication often requires uncovering a family's underlying issues.

Difficulty can also occur when in-laws from families with different communication styles are brought into your family. Like her family, the young bride is used to a lot of teasing because to her it shows love and intimacy, but her husband is not familiar with being teased in that manner. When she makes fun of him, however good-natured she may be about it, he becomes hurt. They have to gain awareness of their different styles and make accommodations to assure mutual comfort.

Crisis Points

Events Impede Communication Life

Cycle crisis points and external events, such as deteriorating economic conditions or a natural disaster, put a strain on communication and make it vulnerable to breaking down altogether.

Major life-cycle events include major moves and job changes, marriage, the arrival of children and grandchildren, empty nesting, divorce, and death. They involve adding people to or subtracting people from the family, which changes the nature of relationships and the way people communicate with one another. Even "good" changes, such as the birth of a child, puts enormous stress on communication patterns.

The growth of a family business, as welcome as it may be, can also strain communication to the breaking point. Growth may simply outpace the communication systems that a family has put in place. When a business starts out, communication is usually very informal. Sammy can just shout across a couple of desks to Maria, or they can talk to each other about the business at home during dinner. But when a business climbs to 25 or 50 or 500 employees, casual communication doesn't work anymore. Instead, the business-owning family finds it has to make a more formal system part of its business infrastructure. That may involve meetings with employees, internal memos, an e-mail system and a company newsletter. Ideally, a formal communication system will clearly state policies about who communicates to whom and when.

Communication Issues

Each Family Member Has Specific Concerns

Resolving conflict thoroughly and improving communication often requires uncovering a family's underlying issues. When family business members start to talk about communication in seminars that we lead, the biggest problem they cite is that there's just not enough communication. When we dig beneath the surface, we find that they feel they're not trusted. "If you're not telling me what's going on, it's because you don't trust me." They feel they're not listened to—again because they're not trusted and they're not taken seriously.

Everyone in a business-owning family has specific issues they deeply care about. As we suggested in Chapter II, a conversation might not be as simple as it appears on the surface. People are often looking for the messages that affect them, or viewing messages through their own special lens. In unraveling the difficulties of communication, it helps to know what people's "hot-button" issues are. They differ some from family to family and individual to individual, but these are typical:

Children (of all ages): Their concerns include having power, at least over their own lives; resolving their identity; gaining confidence and self-esteem and, not surprisingly, being loved by their parents. These issues don't go away in adulthood. Even grownups need external affirmation from their childhood authority figures, usually their parents. A parent can be direct and say, "That was a great job. You're wonderful." A parent can also be abusive, hitting the child and yelling, or severely neglecting him. To the child, the abuse is the way his parent communicates love, so the grownup child communicates in the same way, not just in his own family but also in the business. Sometimes just helping a person to recognize that they're perpetuating an ineffective pattern is enough to motivate them to change. Consider Cheryl, who recently was promoted to a senior management position in her family's company. At first, she adopted a style of yelling at employees and berating them when she thought they'd done something wrong. After all, that's how her father treated employees and how he kept her in line and pushed her toward excellence when she was growing up. She thought such toughness would bring respect. But soon, some of the best employees in her division began to leave. Finally, a concerned board member took her aside and told her that her belligerent communication was alienating her employees. Maybe, he suggested, she could be more effective if she adopted a communication style that was different from her father's. Cheryl got the message and began to learn more constructive approaches toward dealing with her staff.

Spouses. The relationship between a wife and husband is probably the most complicated relationship there is. A big issue for spouses is the ability to be oneself with one's husband or wife. People often look to a spouse to compensate for their childhood issues and a spouse responds by unwittingly playing many roles: parent, child, sibling, cousin, even childhood friend. Ideally, a spouse is both an independent person and partner—not a stand-in for one's mother or older brother.

In-laws. The major issue with in-laws is whether or not they're part of the family. In a simple example, if a daughter-in-law is excluded from a family photograph, it can communicate to her that she's not really seen as a part of her husband's family. The senior generation walks a delicate balance when it comes to sons- and daughters-in-law. Any appearance of favoritism toward one in-law may be resented by another, or make the other feel excluded. Even more complicated, show your daughter-in-law too much affection and your son—her husband—may feel you love her more than you love him.

Inactive family members and non-owning family members. The issue is the same for both: "Am I a member of the family?" Family members who don't work in the business or who don't own shares in it often worry that they are not regarded as full-fledged members of the family. Frequently, family members work in the business even when they'd be happier elsewhere or retain their shares, because they fear that if they worked elsewhere or sold their shares, they would lose their place in the family. Unfortunately, in some business-owning families, nonactive family members are in fact seen as less important than those who work in the business.

Unraveling the complex issues that lie beneath a family's conflicts is generally something that a family cannot do by itself. Outside professional help is usually needed. We talk about that more in Chapter VII.

Other Impediments to Good Communication

There are still other factors that make communication difficult.

For one thing, we don't always say what we mean. Sometimes, as you have seen, we intentionally avoid saying what we mean to protect others or ourselves. But other times, unintentionally, what we say is ambiguous. As a result, you mean one thing but the person you're talking to hears something else. "You said to be on the corner at half past!" "But I meant half past one, not half past two!"

Family members who don't work in the business or who don't own shares in it often worry that they are not regarded as full-fledged members of the family.

Sometimes the problem lies with the recipient. We may misinterpret or misperceive what someone else says. For example, your father, the CEO asks, "Don't you think it's a good idea to go call on Don Smith?" He's referring to an important customer. Because your father is the boss, you're likely to interpret that question as an order, not a question. If your brother, whose status is equal with yours in the company, asked the same question, you would be more likely to regard it as a question and tell him what you think. The more power you have, the more likely it is that your questions are perceived as orders. And that can be a dangerous thing! ("What would you think if we opened a second store?" "Don't you think we ought to give plastic extrusion a try?" "Shouldn't we have our own private jet?") At the same time, if you have a history of being taken care of (financially or emotionally), the more likely your questions will be interpreted as a plea for hope.

Another factor that makes communication difficult is that family members get locked into roles and communicate with one another based on those roles.

There's room for all kinds of other misperceptions in a family business. "Maybe it's time you got a master's degree," a brother in a company tells his younger sister. "What's do you mean?" she bristles. "You want me out of the company for a few years while you curry favor with Dad and get promoted?" (She may be using body language to suggest her response.) What her brother really meant was that with a master's degree, she would be more valuable to the company and could enhance her own position. But she jumped to a negative conclusion before sounding him out. That's something we often do in families, based on experiences that go back to our childhood.

Another factor that makes communication difficult is that family members get locked into roles and communicate with one another based on those roles. A husband may need a dependent wife and she may want a strong husband. He can't communicate any uncertainty or let her know if anything is going wrong in the company because he's afraid she'll think something is wrong with him or that she'll break down. She can't exhibit any real strength because she knows he depends on her to look up to him.

CEOs, too, get locked into roles. A CEO may find it hard to communicate with others in the company because she doesn't want to convey any self-doubt. She knows hundreds of employees rely on her. She fears that if she shares personal information they may view her less as the "boss," and this might lead to them worrying that there are problems in the company. For her, it's just too risky.

Being locked into roles not only places a heavy burden on people—it also curbs honest, open communication.

Be Aware of the Traps

As you can see, the road to good communication is an extremely bumpy one. As previously discussed, it is filled with hazards:

EXHIBIT 3

9 Common Pitfalls in Communication

1. Fear that communication will make things worse.

2. Life crisis points, such as marriage, birth, and death.

3. Family patterns of communication and conflict cycles.

4. Being locked into a role.

5. Misinterpreting what someone else says.

6. Multiple levels of communication: verbal, body language and parallel conversations.

7. Fear that others in the family are too fragile to discuss tough issues.

8. Hidden personal issues, such as need for parental love or to be a full-fledged family member.

9. Fear of an emotional response.

Once you become aware of these traps, you can take action. That may mean discussing, before the wedding, how you and your future spouse will handle the differences in the conflict cycles of your families of origin or their styles of communication. It may mean initiating an effort to understand the deep-seated issues that affect your family as a whole and the members within it.

Most of all, it means taking the steps to improve communication in your family—so that you and other family members can all become more skilled at interacting with one another and managing your conflicts.

Improving communication begins with you. The next chapter will be your guide.

Take the steps to improve communication in your family—so that you and other family members can all become more skilled at interacting with one another and managing your conflicts.

IV. Improving Your Communication Skills

The famous Gucci clan went down in flames as a business-owning family when the Italian-based company was sold in 1993. In her book, *The House of Gucci*, Sara Gay Forden tells the story of how the international luxury goods company both thrived and suffered at the hands of its volatile owners, whose inability to communicate aggravated their serious legal problems and turf wars.

Consider Aldo Gucci, a second-generation leader, and his son, Paolo. Aldo was a tough and domineering father. Paolo, a creative man who struggled unsuccessfully to get his ideas heard and gain some influence in the family business, was fired from the company instead. In one confrontation, Aldo asked Paolo to side with him against Aldo's brother and partner, Rodolfo.

"How can you expect me to help you with Rodolfo when you won't even let me breathe?" Paolo responded. Aldo swore savagely at Paolo, flung an ashtray at him, and screamed: "You are crazy! Why don't you do what I tell you?"

Aldo's idea of communication was that he would issue orders and others would do as he said. Even when Paolo was nearly 50 years old, his father still expected blind obedience.

Healthy communication can often prevent the misunderstandings around which conflicts occur.

Enraged at what he felt was his family's unfair treatment, Paolo vowed to bring down the house of Gucci. He investigated the company's finances and filed lawsuit after lawsuit. As a result, his father at age 81 was sentenced to prison for a year for tax evasion and Paolo's cousin, Maurizio, was forced for a time into exile from Italy. In 1987 Paolo sold his small stake in the company in a transaction that would eventually lead to putting the control outside the family.

In many ways, Paolo was like Sally Bingham. Feeling that he was not listened to and believing he was treated unfairly; he became a whistle-blower who brought the family to its knees.

The Guccis and the Binghams offer extreme examples of how conflict and the failure of communication contribute to the fall of a business-owning family. They are also examples of avoidable tragedy. Only through sound communication do conflicts get satisfactorily resolved. Healthy communication can often prevent the misunderstandings around which conflicts occur.

A Communication Inventory

One way to begin improving communication skills—yours and your family's—is to take stock. Conduct an "inventory" of how well your family communicates. You can usually sense when communication is going well or when it isn't. Certain tangible signs, however, will confirm your instinctive feelings. Indications that communication falls short of what it could be are:

—Lack of eye contact.

—Unresponsiveness to questions or inquiries. For example, one family member does not return another's calls or delays the response.

When communication is going well, it is a sign that a lot of other things are going well.

—Unproductive meetings. People switch subjects or compete for control of the discussion. Serious questions are glossed over. Cues that others want to talk—the opening of a mouth to speak or a raised hand—are ignored.

—Distrust of one another.

—Hidden agendas.

—Communicating through others.

—Frequent blaming of others.

Signs that communication in a family is constructive include:

—Plenty of eye contact.

—Quick response to phone calls and inquiries.

—Good meetings. The amount of time that people talk is fairly equal.

—Trust and caring.

—Honest expression of disagreement.

—Direct communication.

—People are enthusiastic and motivated.

—Family members exhibit self-confidence.

—Family members are informed about important family and business matters.

When communication is going well, it is a sign that a lot of other things are going well, too. Family members love and trust one another. They are more generous and altruistic toward one another. They are more caring and open.

If your communication inventory suggests some real problems, you need to take action as quickly as possible, possibly calling in outside professional help.

Even when communication works well, however, there is always room for improvement. No family is perfect and we all slip into poor communication modes from time to time. Families are most vulnerable to communication mishaps during times of stress and the scars of bad communication can be avoided. Most of us need to hone and re-hone our communications skills and to be reminded that we can't learn too much about how to communicate.

Where To Start

The best place to begin is with yourself. **When you improve your own communication, the changes you make will tend to make those around you change, too.** They won't be able to respond to you in the same old annoying, unproductive ways. You'll be like the pebble thrown into the pool, creating a ripple effect. Here are some surefire steps for enhancing your own skills and, in turn, raising the overall level of communication in your family and your business:

1. Learn to listen well. Listening well means being respectful of what others are saying and making a genuine effort to understand them. Management consultants Mardy Grothe and Peter Wylie say that listening requires four skills:

- **Attending.** This means using good body language to show that you're following—and interested in—what the other person has to say. For example, lean forward and look people in the eye when they're talking to you. Nod now and then to encourage them. Avoid negative body language, like rolling your eyes at the ceiling or slamming your palms down on the table. In general, within your family, show attention using the patterns your family uses to demonstrate concern and interest.

- **Asking thought-provoking questions.** These are questions that invite the other person to think out loud. Avoid yes or no questions.

- **Encouraging.** If the topic is a touchy one, the other person may hold back. You need to encourage him or her to keep talking. You can say something like: "It's important for me to hear what you have to say." But do not relate a story about yourself to show you understand, because often you don't. Allow them to speak until they feel heard.

- **Reading back.** When you "read back," you summarize in your own words what the other person has been saying. Doing so let's other people know you are really trying to listen and gives them a chance to correct any misunderstandings.

According to Grothe and Wylie, these four listening skills send an important message: "I care enough about you and our relationship to try to really hear what you're saying to me." A lot of frustrated business owners say, "Why don't you just *listen* to me?" Like Aldo Gucci, they make the mistake of equating listening (yours) with doing what they want you to do. Real listening doesn't require obedience or even agreement. Think of it as a tool for gaining understanding and solving problems—or for enjoying your relationships with others.

2. Avoid misinterpreting others or being misinterpreted. Remember that communication takes place on many levels at once, so take time to detect what's going on. If you feel someone has just demeaned you, you don't have to go on the attack. Play things back and try to determine whether a perceived put-down was really intended. Ask questions and check things out. If the other person really did intend a slight, direct your response to the behavior instead of attacking the person. Depending on the situation, an appropriate response might be: "Even if you think you know what I'm about to say, you need to allow me to finish my sentence." Or, "I really am interested in hearing what Joyce has to say. Please don't interrupt." If someone has just attacked something you said, you might say: "Well, that's a very interesting point of view, but it doesn't really address what I just said."

When you say something and the listener responds in a way that surprises you—with anger, for example—check to see if you miscommunicated. Find out what the other person heard. Is it what you thought you said? If not, could you have delivered your message differently so that what you intended is what was heard?

Real listening doesn't require obedience or even agreement.

It's also important to ask, "Am I being honest with myself?" Did you, in fact, want to make the other person angry but to appear innocent of your intent? If the answer to such self-questioning is, "No, I wasn't being honest with myself," or, "The other person heard a message different from the one I sent," you know you have room to improve your communication.

Make it your job to be explicit. Suppose, for example, that you are in the more powerful position. As we suggested in Chapter II, you may have to make extra effort to have your questions perceived as questions rather than as orders. It's not enough to say, "What do you think about calling on this client?" That will be seen as a dictate. Instead, you'll need to preface your question: "I'm really looking for your opinion. This is not an order. What do you think about calling on this client? Is that a good idea or a bad idea?"

3. Build and maintain trust. To resolve conflict and create a good environment for communication, you must have trust. However, trust is often considered a "chicken-or-egg" issue, raising such questions as: "Can you build trust without good communication? Can you have good communication without trust?" Our answer is: Don't worry about where you jump into it. You've got to jump into it somewhere. **If you're the one who is trying to make positive change in a relationship, it's important to act as if there is trust even if there isn't. Behaving as if trust exists will actually help build trust.**

The best ways to create trust are to be trustworthy yourself and to extend trust

The best ways to create trust are to be trustworthy yourself and to extend trust to others.

to others. Do what you say you will do and be consistent so that over time, others know they can rely on you. People need to be able to predict your behavior and understand it. Inconsistent behavior not only creates distrust, it engenders a lack of self-confidence in others. You can destroy a lifetime of trust-building very quickly by doing something that's inconsistent with your behavior.

EXHIBIT 4 ▐███████████████████████████

Trust Axiom

Generosity builds trust, secrecy destroys it.

- Financial
- Information
- Time
- Spirit
- Love, caring and nurturance

The point of the Trust Axiom above is that, **to build trust, you have to be generous in all five dimensions—not just generous with money but generous about providing information, giving your time, giving of yourself and being fully present when you are with another by offering love and care.** If you are generous in only one area—money, for example—others may begin to feel that you have a hidden agenda, perhaps a desire to control them or an expectation of a favor.

We all have a tendency at one time or another to say, "I don't trust you." That's a blanket statement that means a lot more than you may intend it to mean. The following Trust Matrix[1] and its 16 boxes should be helpful to you in narrowing down what you mean when you think you don't trust someone in your family business.

---

[1]This matrix was developed with Wharton's Enterprising Families Initiative director Timothy G. Habbershon.

EXHIBIT 5 ████████████████████████████████

Trust Matrix

(name)	Individual	Team	Family	Company
Honesty				
Intentions				
Skills & Abilities				
Communication				

Suppose you think you don't trust your brother, Victor. Consider each of the traits on the left—Honesty, Intentions, Skills & Abilities and Communication—and evaluate Victor's reliability in each of the situations across the top of the matrix. Honesty refers to being truthful. Intentions refer to whether the other person has their own interests at heart or the interests of others. Skills and Abilities mean do they have the skills and abilities to do their job or function effectively in the relevant group they are in. Communications means do they tell you what you need to know when you need to know it. When "Perhaps Victor's honest with me when we are in a one-on-one situation, but when we get into another setting, such as the company or the family, it's like he's speaking out of the other side of his mouth. Perhaps I find that his intentions are good everywhere but in a team, where he tends to use the team for his own benefit without giving much back. Maybe I'll realize that his skills and abilities are good across the board, and that he communicates well everywhere but in the family."

This exercise will give you an understanding of Victor's traits (or those of any other family member) that give you pause. You'll see that the statement "I don't trust you" is too broad. You probably don't distrust Victor 100 percent; you distrust him only a little in just one or two boxes, perhaps 5 or 10 percent.

If Victor has a high level of self-confidence and the two of you don't have a great deal of conflict with each other, you might be able to easily discuss with him what you learned.

What if you lack confidence in your sister's skills and abilities in the company? You might say to her: "You're a great family member. I love you as a sister. I think your intentions are good, but I just don't think you can get the job done. Look at all these ways I trust you. Now let me be honest about what your abilities and skills are and why I see it this way. I might be wrong, but we need to discuss this." That's more productive than saying, "I don't trust you and Mom and Dad don't trust you."

One more thing before we leave the subject of trust: It's important to recognize any damage you may have inflicted that has led to the deterioration of trust and to accept responsibility and offer to make up for it. This often requires more than just a simple apology. Doing so is less costly than staying in an environment where trust is lacking.

4. Allow others to be emotional in your presence without shutting them down. Withhold your own desire to say something to stop them or even to comfort them. The best thing you can do when others are in tears or in a rage is to give them the space to be emotional without judging them.

Faced with someone else's emotions, most of us get uncomfortable and do what we do when we see something on television that we don't like: we try to "change the channel" by changing the subject. We may say something like, "You're over-reacting," or "You're too emotional. That's why I don't talk to you." We may even attempt something soothing, like, "It's not so bad. Look on the bright side." Such responses tell the other person that you're denying his emotions or that you believe he is feeling the "wrong" things." They also send the message that you can't handle the emotionality and that, therefore, you can't be present for him and in some senses that you can't be trusted.

You may want to avoid raising a difficult issue because you dread the other person's reactions. But you should bring the issue up and let the other person yell, scream or cry. Maybe the two of you can't talk about the issue this time. You may need to wait a few weeks or a few months and raise the issue again. There may be more hurt and anger but you would be smart to just listen. Yelling, screaming, and tears are part of the process. Eventually, the other person will see that you accept his or her emotions and you will be able to have a conversation about what troubles you.

EXHIBIT 6

Ten Comments That Shut Down Communication

1. "You're too emotional. No wonder I never talk to you."

2. "Why don't you just snap out of it?"

3. "It's not as bad as you think."

4. "I understand what you are going through; let me tell you a story about myself."

5. "You're just like your (mother, father, brother, etc.)."

6. "You're acting like a child."

7. "See! That's just what I knew you'd say!"

8. "Why can't you be more logical?"

9. "You ought to know better than that."

10. "How do you think I feel?

5. Regard disagreements as emotionally "neutral." This may sound like it contradicts the previous point, but it does not. Regarding disagreements as emotionally neutral is an ideal—we can't all reach it but it helps to try. What it means is that family members have all worked through their issues with one another in a process that includes allowing others to be emotional. In other words, they have taken away the emotional issues because they have worked them out. They can now regard any disagreement or conflict as being just another opinion or another problem that they have to solve.

In good communication, the honest expression of disagreement is devoid of emotional content. There are no hidden meanings or oblique messages or hurt feelings or distrust. Under such conditions, you can express disagreement without worrying that you're showing disrespect for someone else, without dreading their reaction, and without fear of reprisal. There's no reason for reprisal. "I know that you're not expressing disagreement because you dislike me. We just have two different opinions. We also have a history of working out our differences in a way that is fair. I have no reason to think that you're going to use this difference as a way to take advantage of me because I know that you have a track record of not trying to take advantage of people. You feel the same way about me. We have removed the emotional content from our disagreement, enabling communication to take place."

> *In good communication, the honest expression of disagreement is devoid of emotional content.*

6. Communicate directly. Family members frequently engage in a process known as "triangulation." This happens when one person uses another person to deliver a message to a third party. Example: Grandma is miffed because her granddaughter, Teri, away at college, didn't call or write to thank her for a birthday present. Grandma confronts Teri's mother instead: "Gee, I haven't heard from Teri. Did she get the birthday present I sent?" Grandma is addressing the wrong person in hopes that her daughter will do the dirty work of confronting Teri for her bad manners. Not only that, Teri's mother will probably feel a sting of rebuke because Grandma, consciously or unconsciously, is sending a message that Teri hasn't been brought up properly. She will likely also feel a pang of guilt because the third point that may be being communicated is that Teri's mother doesn't care about Grandma enough and this situation is her responsibility. In a sense, Grandma is demanding that Teri's mother take the responsibility for seeing to it that Teri responds to the gift. It's a situation destined to stir up anger and ill feelings.

In the first place, Grandma shouldn't triangulate. But it is also important not to let oneself be used to deliver someone else's messages. Teri's mother could say something like, "I don't know if she's received your gift, Mom. Why don't you send her an e-mail and ask? You know she always loves hearing from you."

Good communication requires taking the responsibility for directly addressing the person you want to receive a message. When you evade that responsibility, you take the risk of creating or escalating hurt feelings and ill will.

7. Search for underlying issues. As said earlier, poor communication in a family is a sign of deep-seated issues that need to be addressed. Uncovering such issues and working them out is an extremely difficult task, one that usually requires the help of an outside professional.

You can begin on your own, however, by putting yourself in somebody else's shoes. Try to understand why they might not like you, why they may have unresolved issues, why they make so much or so little of what you say. Is it something about yourself, something about the other person, or both? Is it something about the situation? Did you have more advantages as a child? Does he carry with him the scars of being mugged as a 14-year-old or of a serious, long-term childhood illness? When you can put yourself in another's position, you can better communicate and work out differences because you understand and appreciate their point of view.

8. Make all your levels of communication consistent with one another. If our actions don't support our words, people begin to distrust what we say. If we say we are interested in the other person's perspective but drum our fingers on the table when he is speaking, our body language is telling him something else. If we tell our employees that our family business is a wonderful, caring place to work but we skimp on salaries and are stingy with sick leave, our employees will conclude this isn't a caring place, no matter what we say. We will risk losing whatever loyalty and extra effort we might have hoped for.

Once you gain more knowledge about the many different ways humans communicate, you can more consciously control your nonverbal messages, recognize and explain them when they are inappropriate, and make them consistent with one another and with your verbal messages. As you do so, others will come to trust you more, laying the groundwork for better communication.

9. Help others build self-confidence. The more self-confidence people have, the better they are at communicating and resolving conflict. But sometimes, there's an imbalance: you may have a great deal of self-confidence while someone you wish to communicate with and have a better relationship with does not. Perhaps you feel that your sister has misunderstood or misperceived you. If her self-confidence is strong, you can go to her and say, "Listen, I think you heard something different than what I said. Can you tell me what you heard? Why do you think I would have said it that way?" Unless there's a real power difference, two equally and reasonably highly self-confident people can usually hash out a miscommunication and come to an understanding.

If you're in a position of considerably greater power or if your sister is lacking self-confidence, however, it is going to be harder to have a direct conversation about the misperception. She will see such a conversation itself as an attack or as an attempt to brainwash or manipulate her.

The more self-confidence people have, the better they are at communicating and resolving conflict.

What you can do is try to help her build self-confidence. Give her more responsibility in the company, in your family council, or in the family's philanthropic decisions. As she succeeds, offer recognition and appreciation—followed by more responsibility. Eventually, as she sees that you take her seriously, her self-confidence will grow and so will the quality of the communication that takes place between the two of you. It is also important to note that a lack of consistent behavior will harm someone else's self-confidence. It is more important that consequences (including rewards) for actions are consistent than that they be of the appropriate level of severity or generosity.

10. Don't be trapped by the past. Are you treating your grownup siblings or your grownup children they way you did when they were children? And vice versa? Are you still holding a grudge over things your brother did when he was 12 or angry with your mother for not giving you enough attention when you were in middle school and she was so involved in the business? Whatever your resentments from the past, it will be helpful to recognize them and make personal adjustments so that you can treat other family members as peers and shake off the roles of the past. Lucy may have been treated as the "smart one" and her sister, Meryl, as the "pretty one" when they were girls. But those labels may have nothing to do with Lucy and Meryl as young women, both of them smart and attractive. But family members may still be regarding one as the smart one and the other as the pretty one—both very limiting perceptions.

Decide to let go of your childhood views of other family members. Get to know them anew, through adult eyes.

Enjoying the Results

Making the effort to improve your own ability to communicate takes courage. You may have to work hard to overcome your own fear of expressing legitimate anger or of risking another person's emotional response when difficult issues are raised. You may have to learn to let others talk more. Whatever your limitations, you have to be willing to change yourself as well as to view others in new ways.

But the results will be obvious when you see how differently conversations can go. Consider these examples:

Example #1:

You are the 27-year-old brother picking up your 23-year-old sister to take her to a company event.

Old Style of Communicating:

YOU: Are you really going to wear THAT?

SISTER (angrily): What's wrong with it?

YOU: You mean what's wrong with your navel showing?

SISTER: Are you afraid I'll get more attention than you?

YOU: You never seem to know what's appropriate!

SISTER: What's that supposed to mean?

YOU: What do you think it means? As usual, you show no judgment. When are you going to grow up?

[ANGER ESCALATES]

New Style of Communicating:

YOU: Yipes! I'm really sorry; I clearly forgot to tell you what kind of a party this is. You're beautiful and I love the look, but if you don't want to be the only one there with a crop top on you'd better change.

SISTER: Why? What's going on? It's just another company picnic.

YOU: No, no. Gosh, I'm sorry; I really needed to pay more attention. It's an upscale garden party. Hey, I'm really sorry about the mix-up. We don't have to hurry so if you want to change we can make the time.

SISTER: Sure. I wish I'd paid more attention.

YOU (on the return of you sister, now wearing an appropriate dress): Hey, you look great! I can't wait to see our customers fawn over you.

Example #2

You are the 55-year-old founder of the family business. You hope that your oldest son, Jamal, 30, will succeed you as CEO someday.

Old Style of Communicating

YOU: Your mother's on my back, telling me you want to go back to college and get a master's degree.

JAMAL: I tried to talk to you about it before, dad, but you wouldn't listen.

YOU: I listened all I needed to. Now you listen to me. This idea is nuts. I need you here.

JAMAL: But I could contribute so much more if I had an MBA—

YOU. Forget about it. Perhaps you weren't listening to me. I said I need you here. I never had a master's degree. You don't need one. But the company needs you.

New Style of Communication:

YOU: You really want to get an MBA? I never had an MBA. Why do you think you need one?

JAMAL: I know you never got one, Dad, and what you've done is fantastic and you don't need one. But you've been telling me you want me to run the company someday, right?

YOU: Yeah, that's been my dream since you were born.

JAMAL: Well, my feeling is that the company is growing so fast that I need certain skills that I can't get without more education. I need to know more about finance and strategy if I'm going to help this company continue to grow.

YOU: But we've done all right. And what would I do without you?

JAMAL: Yes, we have done all right. I know you need me here. But we can work something out. I could take an executive MBA and go to school on weekends. There may be some other alternatives. Also, you don't need me as much now as you will in the future and I just want to be in the best position to take care of things.

YOU: Okay. Tell you what. Let's set aside some time this weekend. You come over to the house and we'll talk it through. I can give it some more thought, too. You've got a point—education is always valuable. It's just that I value you so much and would hate to lose you working by my side.

Did you notice in each example how, when you changed your own way of communicating, the response of the other party was entirely different? In the first instances, trust seems lacking, and false assumptions are made about each other. Unfortunately, people seem to be in a rut left over from childhood.

But when "you" change your style of communication, you take responsibility for the problem and demonstrate your trust for the other person. When the new style is used, the other person has confidence that you are acting in the best interests of all concerned and real communication can take place.

This chapter has suggested many ways in which you can take responsibility for improving your own communication. In the next chapter, we look at ways a whole family can work together to create an environment that supports communication that works.

> *When "you" change your style of communication, you take responsibility for the problem and demonstrate your trust for the other person.*

V. Creating a Climate for Good Communication

While taking individual responsibility for good communication is essential, what a business-owning family can do as a group to improve communications offers almost unlimited possibilities. A family makes

When family members support each other's efforts to improve their interactions, they can reach the goal much faster than they could alone.

a very powerful statement to family members and to employees when it commits itself as a whole to bettering, in a rigorous and disciplined manner, the way it communicates. Doing so helps individual family members strengthen their resolve to become more effective communicators and gives them hope in an area where they may have seen only hopelessness before. When family members support each other's efforts to improve their interactions, they can reach the goal much faster than they could alone.

Taking a Systems Approach

It's helpful to take a *systems* approach—that is, to think in terms of creating an environment that encourages and supports real communication taking place. One way to begin is for the family to appoint a Communications Committee. A small family can ask two individuals to serve in this capacity while a larger one can choose three or more. Assign the committee to do an inventory of the family's communication as a whole, looking at its strengths and weaknesses. The committee should take care not to place blame for any weaknesses since doing so may cause some family members to not participate.

Based on what it finds, the committee can develop a plan of action for shoring up communication throughout the family and between the family and the business. Ideally, the committee presents its proposed plan to the family or its elected representatives (a family council) for adoption. By accepting the plan, the family commits itself to doing the work necessary to make good communication become a reality.

The committee can develop a plan of action for shoring up communication throughout the family and between the family and the business.

A plan of action could include some or all of the following elements:

Education of Family Members. Many business families find it useful to invite experts to lead sessions on communication at family meetings or retreats. This way, family members can learn better communication skills while together and help one another practice what they've learned. Topics might include better listening, conflict resolution, negotiating, trust building, teaching children how to communicate, running meetings effectively, and anger management.

When communication education is made a part of family meetings, family members begin to understand that learning to communicate better is a high priority and that it is a life-long, ongoing process. It's not just a one-shot deal. Each education session reinforces what family members have learned before and takes them a step farther.

Regular Communication. Every family can benefit from regularly scheduled conversations. By instituting meetings and forums in which family members can talk with one another, a family creates a system for dealing with miscommunication as well as more serious conflict on an ongoing basis instead of letting disagreements fester until they explode into open hostility.

When it comes to how often family members should meet, "one size does not fit all." It depends on the family's communication style. In the context of the business, a weekly meeting works well for many families. However, if members of your family tend to interrupt one another many times a day, it would be better to meet more often, perhaps daily. Then, instead of interrupting others

Family councils, family meetings, and family retreats all provide a way for the family to talk on a regularly scheduled basis.

while they're working, family members can save comments and questions and other issues for the regularly scheduled communication. That forces family members to prioritize, and it means they interrupt only for matters of extreme importance. Keep in mind that interruptions can be a source of friction in relationships. They communicate the message that "I'm more important than you are," or, "What I have to talk about is of the highest priority," even though it may not be.

Family councils, family meetings, and family retreats all provide a way for the family to talk on a regularly scheduled basis. However, it's also important to keep informal lines of communication open through fun events, like family dinners, vacations and family reunions that involve the whole family. Some families also find it helpful and fun to have a newsletter that can be sent to everyone via e-mail in between meetings and get-togethers. These are particularly good ways to distribute photographs and inform the family of important events, like birthdays, graduations, and weddings.

Third-Party Assistance. Conflicts run so deep in some families that family members just can't find their way out without outside help. In such cases, the

Communication Committee might recommend, in its action plan that professional help be brought in to help the family sort out its issues and engage in a process that will put it on the road to better communication. We need to stress, that if your family is troubled, outside help is mandatory because self-doctoring can make things worse.

In families that are less troubled, the committee can spell out the conditions for turning to a third party. It can recommend, for example, that a trusted and skilled family friend be asked to help resolve certain differences. It might also recommend that a professional consultant be brought in to help the family deal with knottier conflicts as well as defining how the consultant is selected and what authority they might have. This way, the family makes a decision about how it will handle conflicts before they occur—not in the heat of battle. If you do this before an explosion, you will be very thankful when the need arises.

Running Effective Meetings. Good meetings need good leaders. The Communications Committee can help the family clarify how meetings should be run and the family's communication education program can help family members develop skills not only in leading meetings but also participating in them productively. Exhibit 7 describes the role of the leader:

EXHIBIT 7

Running an Effective Meeting

Chair controls the meeting and makes sure that:

- People talk uninterrupted and not for too long

- People don't go off topic unless all agree

- Decisions are reached through a pre-agreed decision making process

- Chair participates at a minimal level

- Encourage examples when people differ

- All have a chance to talk

- Help others see boundary between family and business issues

Note that one of the chair's responsibilities is to curb people who talk too long, get off the subject, or behave inappropriately in other ways. When choosing a meeting chair, it's best to select someone who enjoys a lot of trust from the others and is the least likely to upset them when they must be asked to get back on the topic or cautioned not to provoke someone else. The chair has input more by how to run the meeting and less by what they say. Some of the most effective chairs we have witnessed rarely offer an opinion.

The question of "whom to include" often comes up with regard to family meetings. The more harmonious your family, the more people you can include. You can't assume that harmony will come about by including everyone, however. The opposite is often true as including everyone creates opportunity for misinterpretations and hurt feelings. When a family is disharmonious, it's best to start out small. Some families begin by including people of one generation who are at a certain level in the company. Over time, they expand the meetings to include children and cousins and in-laws.

As a general guideline, always remember that the difference between a nuclear explosion and a nuclear reaction is how the energy is contained. If the emotional energy of the family cannot be contained in a large gathering, make the group a size where the energy can be contained.

Rules for Communication. Some business families develop policies that cover both internal and external communications. In the beginning, however, it's best just to set forth a few rules so that they can be readily remembered and practiced. The rules might include such issues as confidentiality, interruptions, how soon family members will return phone calls from one another, who can talk on behalf of the company or family and when and who can family members talk to within the company. Sometimes they include a "code of conduct," outlining how family members should treat one another. They might also adopt the items listed in Exhibit 8 on team behavior:

EXHIBIT 8

Good Advice for Team Behavior

- Respect others and demonstrate respect.

- Understand when to interfere and when not to.

- Know everyone's goals and be open.

- Tolerate differences.

- Listen.

- Remember the Trust Axiom: Generosity builds trust but secrecy destroys it.

Recognizing Family Patterns. The Communication Committee's work can include a look at the family's communication patterns and how they help or hinder the family. The committee should be encouraged to make recommendations to the family about which patterns to reinforce, which ones to change or eliminate, or new patterns that could enhance the family and its business.

The family's patterns would make a good subject for one of those family meeting education sessions. One way to introduce the topic would be to show the film, "My Big Fat Greek Wedding." It's a romantic comedy in which, a young woman from a big, boisterous business-owning family of Greek origin falls in love with a mild-mannered schoolteacher, the only child of a quiet, restrained couple who are definitely not Greek. The differences in communication styles of the two households are clear and humorous and can kick off lively discussion among family members.

Another way to become more conscious of patterns of communication is, with the aid of a facilitator, to ask family members in one generation to write down some of the patterns that they perceive. Responses might be:

- "Mom often says, `you know what your father thinks,' when she doesn't want to admit to herself or others her opinions or feelings."

- "Uncle Bob really listens well and makes me feel like he takes me seriously. I wish the other members of his generation were more like him."

- "We argue all the time."

- "We never argue. It's forbidden. So things that ought to be talked about often don't get talked about."

- "If I express my own opinion, Dad thinks I'm disrespecting him."

- "We talk all the time."

- "We disagree a lot but nobody takes it personally."

- "We often go through Mom when we really want to say something difficult to Dad."

- "It's hard to talk with our cousins because our parents are so distrustful of their parents—and vice versa. We always feel like we have to take sides with our parents."

Family members can discuss what they have written down with the whole group and start to pinpoint the communication patterns that work and those that don't. Family can also tell stories of where a communication pattern failed and the family can study it like a case to find lessons. Then they can begin to work on necessary changes.

Raising the Children. A business family's action plan can also include attention to rearing the youngest family members to be good communicators. Parents of the next generation can participate as a group in communication education sessions at family meetings. When the children become old enough, they can join in the family's communication training activities.

In addition to encouraging the development of good communication skills, parents need to let—and to teach—their children to express anger in healthy ways from a very early age. Too often, for the first 12 years of their lives, children have no opportunity to express hostility with their parents (parents too often don't realize that they have inadvertently communicated to their children that anger is not tolerated). They're too afraid. Then, sometime between ages 12 and 17, they realize they can express hostility and they often have 12 to 17 years' worth of anger built up—even if it's just low-level, daily-basis anger. If the parents won't allow children to let it out, the children all too often vent their hostility in passive-aggressive, usually self-destructive, ways. They may reason, "I know you love me but you're not listening to me. Therefore, I have to hurt myself or others to force you to pay attention and listen to me." To get parents to listen, they pierce themselves, shoplift, eat too much or too little, or engage in any of a wide range of unhealthy activities. Often, a child's level of self or other directed hostility is related to two things: How hostile they need to get to cause their parents to listen, and how much anger towards their parents they have built up over the years.

If you can allow your children to express anger in healthy ways—that is, without violence—in their first 12 years, it is likely that the teenage years will go more smoothly. If you give them an opportunity to let off steam and if you talk with them early on about conflict, chances are they won't have to bottle up that 12 to 17 years' worth of rage that will explode in the teenage years. It's tough for parents to do but it's helpful, even if parents can't give the children what they want (that new toy or to stay up late). It's much like letting others express emotion in your presence (as we talked about in Chapter IV). Allowing children to air their grievances, even if you can't change things, lets them know you're listening to them and regarding them as real people.

If you are in the unenviable state of having the teenage child who is just starting to express their hostility, you may want to allow them to and actually encourage it. Do not say "I was an awful parent." Or, "You are wrong and that's not at all true." Rather, listen to your child and encourage them with statements like, "I can see how you'd feel that way." If you are really listening, and not afraid that your child will leave you, you will listen deeply and know what to say. Treat them like an upset best friend, and not like your child upon which so many of your hopes and dreams rest. If you do this and they are highly angry, soon after their outburst, they will feel guilt and will likely apologize. The apology can be accepted, but you should also thank your child and compliment them on the trust in you that they communicated by being so truthful and forthcoming.

Communicating with and in the Business. The Communication Committee can assess not only how family members communicate with one another in the family but how the family's communication impacts the business.

In his published memoir, George G. Raymond Jr. describes how even after his authoritarian father retired from the family business and George Jr. was named CEO, the question of who really was in charge seemed to be an issue with employees.

"During that period, Dad would go to an officer of the company and, just out of curiosity, ask him a question, and the officer would take it as an order and do whatever he thought my father had asked him to do. As a result of this confusing practice by all the top executives, which really went on for five or six years, The Raymond Corporation wobbled. . . It was no coincidence that business, generally, started improving when managers realized that I was, in fact, the boss, and they didn't have to worry about what my father might think or say regarding any action they had taken at my direction."

The Communication Committee can assess not only how family members communicate with one another in the family but how the family's communication impacts the business.

To keep the Greene, New York, material-handling equipment manufacturer prospering, George Jr. eventually found he had to change the company communication system from one that reflected his father's style of managing by instilling fear in employees to one that was open and participative.

As the Raymond story suggests, the Communication Committee needs to explore such issues as: Does the business need a new system of communication as a result of a leadership succession? Is the communication system changing to keep pace with the growth of the business? If the company has gotten so large that the CEO can no longer keep employees informed on a one-on-one basis the way he or she used to, have other methods of communication been put in place to keep employees in the know? Do the company's vehicles of communication—meetings, newsletters, memos, e-mails, etc.—appropriately convey that the owners care about the employees? Do the owners back up that message with action? Can non-family employees be direct with owners without fear of reprisal? Do family members listen adequately to non-family employees? These are some of the questions a family needs to ask and re-ask as it seeks to move its company forward.

Communicating with Shareholders. The family will want to be sure that there is an adequate system for communicating with shareholders—including minority shareholders, non-family shareholders, and shareholders who do not work in the business. Three questions need to be considered: 1) What is told to them, 2) How often (and what is regular and what is more "news" oriented), and 3) How do they communicate with the company? Don't underestimate the power of the minority shareholder—remember the Gucci and Bingham stories.

A Major Goal

In a well-functioning communication environment, people communicate directly with one another. They don't go through other people. However, you

In a well-functioning communication environment, people communicate directly with one another.

have to have good relationships to sustain direct communication. As family members individually and as a group seek to improve their interactions, they will want to work toward increasing direct communication. In a family business, there are four requirements for sustainable direct communication:

1. Individuals able to sustain communication. This requires maturity and, as discussed in the last chapter, a solid amount of self-confidence. Individuals need to be self-aware—that is, to be honest with themselves, to understand their own motivations and desires when they communicate, and to understand what it is they are trying to get across when they communicate.

2. Relationships able to sustain communication because there's mutual trust. If I tell you something directly, you are going to respect it. You are not going to take it as something that's meant to hurt your feelings but as something that's aimed at being beneficial, even if it's criticism. I will regard anything you tell me directly in the same way. We each see that the other has a record of trustworthiness and we are confident that we can be open and honest with each other without harm coming to one or the other. We have unyielding faith that we each have each other's best interests at heart.

3. The family being able to support direct communication. Family members restrain themselves from being overprotective of others' feelings. In a typical pattern, a father and son are talking but Mom jumps in and tries to shut down the communication because she fears someone's feelings will get hurt. To support direct communication, family members have to allow it to happen even if it makes them uneasy. Likewise, people do not talk for others; they encourage everyone to talk for themselves.

4. The whole system—family and business—being able to support direct communication. This is an ideal that is seldom reached, but it's important to strive for. More often than not, the family is not able to support open communication, so it does not occur in the business. Even when the family can communicate openly, non-family senior employees often can't tolerate it. In the best of all possible worlds, everyone in both the business and the family is capable of open communication and the need for the family to present a united front disappears.

Creating a climate that supports good communication is an ongoing process. Though perfection in communication may be out of reach—we all backslide and make mistakes—continuous improvement is an attainable goal, made even more achievable when all family members commit themselves to better communication and participate in the process.

VI. Using Communication To Manage Conflict

Surveys indicate that the more generations a business has been in the family, the more likely the family reports having family conflict regarding the business. One reason is that having more family members involved in the business means a greater number of differing perspectives, increased complexity in communications, and more opportunities for disagreement.

The best way to manage conflict is to address issues long before they explode into hostility.

What the research also suggests, however, is that families that have been in business longer have learned how to express their conflict more and to destigmatize it: "We have learned to live with it, manage it and resolve it, so we are more willing to admit it in surveys and elsewhere." The first generation in a family business views conflict as failure, but later generations recognize that it's acceptable to have conflict and to admit that they do. For them, it is no longer socially desirable to lie by saying, "We don't have any conflict!"

The best way to manage conflict is to address issues long before they explode into hostility. Using the new skills outlined in the two previous chapters, your family can do this.

In an earlier book in the **Family Business Leadership Series**©, we urged family business owners to put policies in place, before the need to address difficult issues arises. When families work out ahead of time how they will handle sensitive questions—like shareholder agreements, compensation, conflict identification and resolution, and criteria for family members who want to work in the business—they stand a better chance of eliminating or reducing future tension. They have already made the decisions when the need was not pressing and heads were cool.

Developing policies, however, requires a great deal of good communication on the part of family members. **Going through the process of developing a policy gives family members valuable experience in communicating. It also helps unify the family by helping them see what values and goals they share and by enlisting their commitment to each other and to the business.** Research shows that ownership unity is necessary to family business success. Unity can only be achieved through conversation.

When Conflict Occurs

A family can't develop a policy for every problem. Conflict and disagreements will inevitably develop. That's a normal part of family business life and is to be expected.

When two people are in conflict, each wants something but their desires don't match or overlap. For example, Curtis wants to be CEO and his sister, Maya, wants to be CEO, but they believe a family business can have only one CEO. Think of their disagreement as two separate circles:

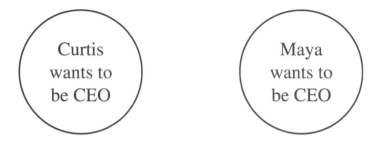

Note that the siblings' circles are very small and so is their range of solutions: There can only be one CEO. When the range of solutions is so narrow, there can only be a winner and a loser—one will become CEO and the other will not.

In many situations, human instinct is to compromise, with each party giving in a little bit. Say Keith wants to expand the business nationally with the family business's products but his equally ambitious brother, Paul, wants to concentrate the business in the region surrounding its headquarters and to develop more products. In a compromise, Keith agrees to test the market in one nearby city instead of the four or five he had hoped for, and Paul agrees to add only one or two new products to one of the company's existing lines instead of starting the whole new product line he dreamed of. Each grumbles to other family members and some non-family executives that the other brother is holding the company back.

What negotiation experts suggest is reframing the discussion. Instead of looking at their conflict as one of who gets to be CEO, Curtis and Maya can draw on their communication skills and through a negotiation process, reframe the problem. They may call on a negotiation consultant to help them. They look for mutual interests and they realize they both want long-term family health and prosperity. They also both want the business to pass on to the next-generation of family members. Recognizing that they have significant interests in common, they begin to brainstorm about the future and enlist other family members to help.

Before long, they have come up with a number of solutions for future leadership that had not occurred to them before. They could run the business as a sibling team. They could hire a non-family CEO and play other important roles— Maya always did like the creative part of the business more than she did management and Curtis is a marketing genius. One could be CEO while the other followed his or her passion.

As they reframe their discussion, Curtis and Maya increase the size of their circles. As their circles expand, they can see where their needs and desires overlap and that more solutions are open to them. The CEO question, as a competitive issue, disappears and brother and sister began to focus on which of the solutions that have been suggested would best meet the goals of long-term family health and business prosperity and continuity.

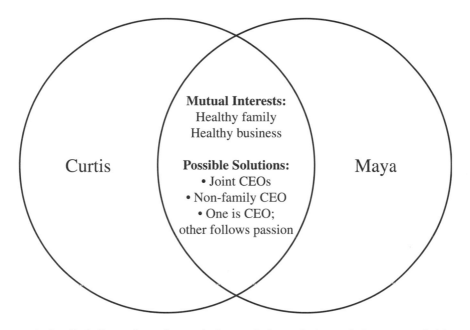

Curtis

Mutual Interests:
Healthy family
Healthy business

Possible Solutions:
• Joint CEOs
• Non-family CEO
• One is CEO;
other follows passion

Maya

A detailed discussion of negotiation techniques is beyond the scope of this book. We recommend reading the classic book, *Getting to Yes: Negotiating Agreement Without Giving In*, by Roger Fisher and William Ury. They point out that often, the ongoing relationship of the parties involved is much more important than the outcome of a particular negotiation. A negotiation, they say, "should produce a wise agreement if agreement is possible. It should be efficient. And it should improve or at least not damage the relationship between the parties."

Fisher and Ury caution against arguing from position—that is, taking a stance and sticking to it ("I want to be CEO"). Your ego gets involved with your position and you develop a stake in "saving face," they warn. Here, briefly, are their four guidelines for negotiating:

1. Separate the people from the problem. Seek to understand reality as the other side sees it and the feelings behind their belief. Recognize that emotions are sometimes more important than talk and can bring talk to an end. Instead of seeing the other person as the problem, try to see yourselves as people with a joint problem. Attack the problem, not the person.

2. Focus on interests, not positions. "Behind opposed positions lie shared and compatible interests, as well as conflicting ones," say Fisher and Ury. Make your own interests known and show appreciation for the interests of the other side—which will make them more open to appreciating yours.

3. Invent options for mutual gain. You want

A negotiation should produce a wise agreement if agreement is possible.

43

to generate a variety of possible solutions before making judgments about them or making a final decision. Seek to dovetail differing interests. Here's where brainstorming becomes useful.

4. Insist that the negotiation be based on objective criteria. Using objective criteria, such as standards of fairness, efficiency, scientific data, market value, and the like, makes the negotiation independent of the will or dominance of either side. It reduces the amount of time spent simply on defending one's own position and attacking that of the other side.

You can see how having some education sessions on negotiation can be helpful to a business-owning family. It's obvious that one of the most important negotiation skills—perhaps THE most important is listening: listening to find out the other party's interests, listening for the other party's point of view and listening for the other party's feelings.

When the Timing Is Right

Remember our discussion of conflict cycles in Chapter II. Each sensitive issue has its own conflict cycle. We get hot about it, we cool down and then we get hot about it again. The time when we most naturally want to resolve conflicts—when they're heating up again—is the worst time to try to resolve them. That is when the people involved are the most verbal about the issue and the most upset. That is also when no one is capable of thinking rationally about the issue and is least able to communicate well. One person tries to keep the conflict from getting out of hand by putting pressure on the other. As a result, emotionalism escalates and so does the conflict.

The best place to try for a resolution is the least natural: when the conflict has cooled down, people are calmer and real communication can take place. We are too afraid at this point to bring up the conflict because we want to avoid ill feelings. Exhibit 9 illustrates the valley of a conflict cycle, showing that the best time to try to resolve a conflict is when a conflict has subsided while the worst time is just when the conflict is warming up again:

EXHIBIT 9 ▮

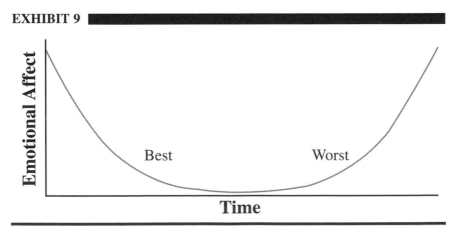

44

One more thing about timing: don't let even small problems fester. They are usually indications of bigger issues. Small problems are only perceived as problems when the things that bind you together become weakened. Even an item as minor as "You never put the cap back on the toothpaste!" can become a big issue when you let it sit too long. The earlier you address a problem, the better. The more you find and address the problems beneath the surface, the better.

A Better Way

"We'd rather sell than have any conflict in this family," is a statement that family business consultants often hear from their clients. In one business-owning family, the members were strongly committed to each other and very involved in one another's lives. Their love and their conviction were real—but their insistence on avoiding conflict made them unable to confront their differences.

"I just want everyone to be happy and to love each other all the time," Mom said. But she could ask penetrating and incisive questions as a board member. What's more, the family had weathered some serious adversity and challenges in the past and had survived them intact and strengthened. It could surely withstand some family disagreement.

With the help of a consultant, family members probed their aversion to conflict. "It's not that it bothers me when we disagree about something," one family member finally said. "Conflict just makes me feel terrible inside."

"You'd rather sell the business and lose all the opportunities it represents—including the common focus and commitment it gives your family—than have to deal with that feeling?" the consultant asked.

"Well, now that you put it that way, maybe it would make more sense for me to learn to cope better with that feeling," she conceded.

"That feeling" became the focus of a family meeting. All admitted to having and fearing "that feeling." All recognized that the ability to honestly confront issues and differences was essential to the family's success as a business-owning team. All committed to work hard on tact and sensitivity, but they also promised to risk experiencing or engendering "that feeling" so that honest dissent would not be suppressed. The family also began to develop an agenda of tough issues, too long avoided, for future family meetings.

No one in the family any longer says they'd rather sell than have conflict. The attitude now is: "We can imagine no family problem so great that we would fail to overcome it, nor any family issue that would make us want to sell our business legacy."

VII. Getting Outside Help

Your family doesn't have to wait until it's in serious trouble to bring in a professional to help with communication. And it shouldn't. The best time to engage a professional is before there's a problem. Even families that communicate well can learn to communicate better. One of the things we find most saddening is when a family too far gone calls for immediate help.

Think of a using a communications professional in much the same way you would think of using an attorney or a management consultant. You want someone to help you prevent problems and make your family business better. Professionals can help families understand their communication patterns and coach family members on communication skills. They can conduct educational sessions or counsel a family on rearing children to be good communicators.

A professional can help you recognize when patterns that work well now won't be functional in the future and assist you in making the necessary changes—for example, helping your family design a communication and conflict system to meet the needs of anticipated growth.

A professional can support a family in its efforts at keeping communication in good working order.

In short, a professional can support a family in its efforts at keeping communication in good working order. That in turn benefits both the family and the business. Interactions become less emotionally draining and more time can be spent enjoying the family and running the company. People in the family and in the business experience greater motivation and commitment.

As suggested earlier, some families need special help. When there's mistrust in the family, family members often miscommunicate or have few conversations and when they have a high level of unresolved conflict, professional assistance is essential. Generally, families can't work out the emotional issues that lie beneath their conflicts by themselves. This process is more about healing families than communicating and it requires sorting out issues that need to be discussed and resolved and those that don't, and helping family members learn how to cope with issues that can't be worked out.

Choosing and Using Professional Help

Professionals who can help business families with conflict and communication come from a variety of fields. You may find one type more appropriate to your situation than another. Here are some of the specialties:

—Family business consultants. They come from a range of disciplines: psychology, management consulting, law, banking, accounting and more. Look for one with solid experience in communication and conflict resolution. The Family Firm Institute, a Boston-based organization of family business professionals, can be helpful. Call FFI at (617) 482-3045 or click on www.ffi.org. In Europe and other parts of the world the association of family companies known as The Family Business Network can also help. FBN can be reached in Switzerland at 41 21 618 02 23 or through the Internet at www.fbn-i.org.

Of course, we at The Family Business Consulting Group, Inc.ˢᵐ would be happy to help you find the right professional. You may contact us at (888) 421-0110 or http://www.efamilybusiness.com.

—Marriage and family therapists. These are mental health specialists trained in psychotherapy and family systems. If you go in this direction, seek a therapist who understands family business dynamics—that is, how the business and the family interact. Contact the American Association for Marriage and Family Therapy in Alexandria, VA.

—Mediators. In mediation, a third-party facilitator helps people discuss difficult issues and negotiate an agreement. The process involves gathering information, framing the issues, developing options, negotiating, and formalizing agreements. For information and referrals, contact the Association for Conflict Resolution in Washington, DC.

Others who can be helpful to you in a search for the right professional include university business schools, especially those that have family business centers or programs; your family business advisors (lawyer, banker, accountant, etc.), and owners of other family businesses. One note of caution: Try to avoid using existing advisors for conflict resolution; it often changes the nature of their advising relationship.

Approach hiring communication and conflict-resolution specialists the same way you would approach hiring any other professional. Find out about their background and experience, how fees are charged and what professional associations they belong to. Obtain references from other clients. Interview several candidates and choose the one that makes the best fit with your family and its needs. Chemistry is crucial and the family should "click" with the advisor. If possible, the choice should be agreed upon by all the family members involved. The choice should not be seen as just the decision of the most powerful family member, such as Mom or Dad or the CEO or of just the most upset family member, like "baby sister."

Getting the Most from a Professional

A family benefits most from working with a communications professional when family members have a real desire to improve what's going on and have faith in the consultant to help them meet their goals.

It's important to stick with the process. When you are trying to make improvements but quit in the middle of the effort, you damage what you were trying to improve. For example, suppose you are redoing the living room in your house and you take the wallpaper off the walls and rip the carpets up. Then you decide you don't want to continue the project. But now the room looks worse than it did before the project began. It's somewhat like that with families. A communication improvement initiative can open up some issues and make people uncomfortable. But stay with it. If you let the communications professional do his or her job and you participate fully in the hard work that's involved, you'll come out the other side with a family that communicates better and is more able to resolve the inevitable conflicts.

VIII. Strategies for Tough Cases

Sometimes, all the communication improvement efforts a family puts in place or all the individual improvements a family member makes just don't seem to make a difference in dealing with a particular family member. When that happens, try not to get frustrated. Instead, develop some coping mechanisms.

First, either as an individual family member or as a coalition within the family recognize that coping is all that you will do and commit yourself to that. Two groups in particular call for a coping strategy: (1) people who just won't change, and (2) members of the older generation.

People Who Refuse To Change

It was clear in one family business that Dad was just never going to change. He was unwilling to be introspective. He thrived on emotional conflict and he loved getting his way and showing his dominance. He was the "silver-back" gorilla of the family: come too close and you get swatted—only, you don't fly a couple of inches, you fly about 30 feet. His son was miserable. However, Dad thought they were communicating just fine. As long as everybody listened to him and did what he said, he figured things were in good shape.

Working with a family business consultant, the son, over a period of several years, learned to communicate with his father in ways that Dad could hear the message without realizing that he was being communicated with. The son learned when to "plant a seed" and when to make a bigger deal of an issue so that some little bit of it would get through. He became skilled in using diversionary tactics—for example, telling Dad they had a problem, presenting a really bad solution and a really good one, and letting Dad make the choice.

In the absence of trust and honesty and a track record for communicating openly, those are the kinds of measures you have to take if you want to remain in the situation and have some effectiveness. It's an entirely different kind of communication, and it doesn't require both sides to participate. It is not ideal, but many believe it is better than no communication at all.

In other cases, siblings might make a pact that they won't get on their father's case every time he embarrasses them because they know he won't change. Then they ignore Dad's behavior or treat it humorously. Sometimes, they talk about it openly. In some families, they just count to 10 and let go of the matter. The tactic depends on the situation and who the difficult person is.

To the extent that you can, the important point is not to let the other person's behavior get to you emotionally. Since it's been established that he or she is not going to change, there is no sense in getting aggravated.

Members of the Older Generation

Communicating with older family members can be difficult for the younger ones. Most of the time, younger people want to impress their parents and grandparents and aunts and uncles rather than to understand them. For their own part, the senior family members don't want to be perceived as forcing their decisions on the younger family members. As a result, instead of talking about themselves and their lives, the older folks tell stories designed to provide "messages" to the younger ones.

A communication breakthrough is most likely to occur when younger family members take the initiative and sincerely invite the older ones to talk, saying, "Don't tell me how I should be. Tell me about YOU. Show me the honest you and don't worry about me thinking less of you. I just want to know more about who you are." Then the younger ones must demonstrate a willingness to listen actively, often many times, to the older people's personal stories and to ask them questions that will draw them out. As young people listen, they learn what issues are important to their elders and develop a language for dealing with them. "The military" might hold special meaning for a grandfather who served during World War II—such as discipline or love of country, protection of a way of life, or simply a set of horrific events that shook them to their own emotional core. Now, because grandchildren in their 20s and 30s are listening to him, they can better understand what he means. They now have ways of communicating that will lead them to feel closer.

In any family, there will be tough cases of one kind or another. They require patience and creativity and a willingness not to let them become emotionally draining to you. Remember, if what you are doing now isn't working, don't keep on doing it! Try something different and know how long you will wait to see success before moving on to something else.

IX. Summary

One man who is given to a hot temper but who is also a good communicator recounts this story: He was coming down the stairs of his home. Angry at his wife, who was in the room at the bottom of the stairs, he started yelling at her and berating her. Suddenly he caught himself. "Why am I talking this way to the person I love most in the world?" he asked himself. He grinned sheepishly at his wife and said, "Mind if I try that entrance again?" He climbed back up the stairs and came back down again, this time expressing his grievance but addressing his wife with love and respect.

Wise business-owning families know that their relationships with each other are more important than their grievances.

Whatever the problem was, he has forgotten it. His relationship with his wife was more important. He understood he was making a mistake and he quickly corrected it.

Wise business-owning families, like this husband, know that their relationships with each other are more important than their grievances. One of the reasons they are in business together is that they want to work together and to enjoy the fruits of their labors as a family.

As much as family members love one another, however, relationships can be difficult. Conflicts arise, many of them as a result of unresolved issues based in childhood: perceived unfairness, the desire to be taken seriously, and so on. Often, a family's ability to resolve its differences is obstructed by its conflict and communication patterns and poor communication skills. Such families will benefit from programs and reading that help them develop sounds tools for communication.

In worst-case scenarios, however, a family is afflicted by lack of trust and honesty, and the desire of some family members to exert power and dominance over others. Communication is not merely inadequate, it is destructive. Families in this situation almost invariably need to turn to outside professional help or admit the situation and leave.

In either instance, individuals can take responsibility for improving their own communication skills. They will be rewarded for doing so because as they improve, others around them will likely change positively in response.

It's even better, however, when all family members commit themselves to improvement, so that they can learn to communicate more effectively with one another and to gain experience and skill in resolving conflicts.

Communication is not a "soft" subject. We have seen, in this book, how lack of good communication and the inability of families to resolve conflict led to the downfall of the Gucci and Bingham dynasties. Countless other family businesses suffer or are lost by families for the same reasons. More significantly, the families themselves are often destroyed when a business is lost in a bitter dispute.

Good communication does more than keep families and businesses going. It is the essence of our relationships. It makes them meaningful and fun and, in the long run, it helps make life worthwhile.

Bibliography

Aronoff, Craig E., Astrachan, Joseph H. and Ward, John L. *Developing Family Business Policies: Your Guide to the Future.* Marietta, GA: Family Enterprise Publishers, 1998.

Aronoff, Craig E. and Ward, John L. *Family Business Ownership: How to be an Effective Shareholder.* Marietta, GA: Family Enterprise Publishers, 2001.

Brenner, Marie. *House of Dreams: The Bingham Family of Louisville*, New York: Random House, 1988.

Fisher, Roger, and Ury, William (with Bruce Patton). *Getting To Yes: Negotiating Agreement Without Giving In*, 2nd edition, New York: Penguin Books, 1991.

Forden, Sara Gay. *The House of Gucci*, New York: William Morrow, 2000.

Grothe, Mardy, and Wylie, Peter. *Problem Bosses: Who They Are and How To Deal With Them*, New York: Fawcett Crest, 1988.

Hamilton, Deborah Brody. "Managing Conflicts and Family Dynamics in Your Family's Philanthropy," *Passages*, an issue paper published by the National Center for Family Philanthropy, July 2002.

Raymond, George G. Jr. *All in the Family...Business: A Personal Memoir and Corporate History*, Chevy Chase, MD: Posterity Press, 2001.

Spencer, Stuart. *The Playwright's Guidebook*, New York: Faber and Faber, 2002.

Tifft, Susan E. and Jones, Alex S. *The Patriarch: The Rise and Fall of the Bingham Dynasty*, New York: Summit Books, 1991.

Suggested Additional Readings

Bingham, Sallie. *Passion and Prejudice: A Family Memoir*, New York: Alfred A. Knopf, 1989.

Ginsburg, Kenneth R., M.D. (with Jablow, Martha M.). *"But I'm Almost 13!"*: *An Action Plan for Raising a Responsible Adolescent*, Chicago: Contemporary Books, 2002.

Tifft, Susan E., and Jones, Alex S. *The Trust: The Private and Powerful Family Behind The New York Times*, Boston: Little Brown and Co., 1999.

Index

The Authors

Joseph H. Astrachan, Ph.D., a principal of The Family Business Consulting Group, Inc.ᵐ, is the Wachovia Chair of Family Business and director of the Cox Family Enterprise Center at Kennesaw State University (Atlanta). He received a lifetime achievement award for his research on family business from the International Family Business Program Association. Astrachan is editor of *Family Business Review*, a scholarly publication of the Family Firm Institute and a contributor to *The Family Business Advisor*.

Kristi S. McMillan, an associate of The Family Business Consulting Group, Inc.ᵐ, is associate director of the Cox Family Enterprise Center, Kennesaw State University (Atlanta). She is active with several professional organizations including the Family Firm Institute and the Association for Conflict Resolution. She is also a founding member of the Georgia Chapter of the Association for Conflict Resolution. McMillan has been a reviewer for *Family Business Review* and has presented her work at professional conferences including the Stetson Family Business Gathering (Stetson University) and the Family Business Forum (Kennesaw State University). She is involved in the 2002 national family business survey sponsored by the Raymond Institute in which she leads the family conflict research component. McMillan's consultations focus on conflict resolution and family business relationship building. Her extensive training includes negotiation and family mediation.